The Don't Laugh Challenge™

11 YEAR OLD EDITION

Don't Laugh Challenge
BONUS PLAY

Join our Joke Club and get the Bonus Play PDF!

Simply send us an email to:

bacchuspublish@gmail.com

and you will get the following:

• **10 BONUS** hilarious jokes!

• **PLUS** an entry in our Monthly Giveaway of a $25 Amazon Gift card!

We draw a new winner each month and will contact you via email!

Good luck!

Welcome to
The Don't Laugh Challenge™

• How do you play?

The Don't Laugh Challenge is made up of 10 rounds with 2 games in each round. It is a 2-3 player game with the players being 'Jester #1', 'Jester #2', and a 'King' or 'Queen'. In each game you have an opportunity to score points by making the other players laugh.

After completing each round, tally up the points to determine the Round Champion! Add all 10 rounds together to see who is the Ultimate Don't Laugh Challenge Master! If you end up in a tie, use our final Tie Breaker Round for a Winner Takes All!

• Who can play the game?

Get the whole family involved! Grab a family member or a friend and take turns going back and forth. We've also added Bonus Points in game 2, so grab a 3rd person, a.k.a 'King' or 'Queen', and earn an extra point by making them guess your scene!

BILLY BOY

The Don't Laugh Challenge™ Activity Rules

- ## Game 1 - Jokes (1 point each)

  Jester #1 will hold the book and read each joke to Jester #2. If the joke makes Jester #2 laugh, Jester #1 can record a point for the joke. Each joke is worth 1 point. At the end of the jokes, tally up your total Joke Points scored for Jester #1 and continue to Game 2!

- ## Game 2 - Silly Scenarios (2 points each + bonus point)

  Without telling the other Jester what the scenarios say, read each scenario to yourself and then get creative by acting it out! You can use sound effects, but be sure not to say any words! If you make the other Jester laugh, record your points and continue to the next scenario.

  BONUS POINT: Get your parents or a third player, a.k.a King or Queen, involved and have them guess what in the world you are doing! Get the King or Queen to guess the scene correctly and you score a BONUS POINT!

The Don't Laugh Challenge ™
Activity Rules

Once Jester #1 completes both games it is Jester #2's turn. The directions at the bottom of the book will tell you who goes next. Once you have both completed all the games in the round, add your total points from each game to the Round Score Page and record the Round winner!

• How do you get started?

Flip a coin. If guessed correctly, then that Jester begins!

Tip: Make any of the activities extra funny by using facial expressions, funny voices or silly movements!

JOKES

WHAT DiD THE PANTS SAY, WHEN ASKED iF THE STORE WAS OPEN?

"SORRY, WE'RE CLOTHES."

_____ /1

HOW MANY LETTERS DOES iT TAKE TO MAKE PEOPLE SMiLE?

ONE. IT'S U.

_____ /1

WHY WAS THE CATERPiLLAR A GREAT ATTORNEY?

SHE REALLY PUT iN THE LEGWORK.

_____ /1

WHY DiD THE CUB JOiN A DEN?

HE COULDN'T BEAR TO BE ALONE!

_____ /1

JOKES TOTAL: _____ /4

12

JESTER 1 CONTINUE TO THE NEXT PAGE ➜

SiLLY SCENARiOS

HEY, ROOSTER! IT'S TiME TO WAKE EVERYONE UP. GET YOUR STRUT ON AND DON'T FORGET TO "COCK-A-DOODLE-DOO!"

/2

BEiNG A BODYBUiLDER BALLERiNA HAS ALWAYS BEEN YOUR DREAM. DANCE YOUR ROUTiNE WHiLE ADDiNG iN THOSE AWESOME MUSCLE FLEXES!

/2

SiLLY SCENARiOS TOTAL: _____ /4

 NOW, PASS THE BOOK TO JESTER 2!

13

JOKES

WHY WAS THE INTERNET BEST FRIENDS WITH THE COMPUTER?

THEY CONNECTED WELL!

____/1

WHY ARE FLOWERS SO POPULAR?

THEY HAVE THE BEST BUDS!

____/1

WHY DID THE SHARKS BECOME FRIENDS?

THEY WERE BOTH VERY CHUMMY!

____/1

HOW DID THE STUDENT FISH BECOME FRIENDS?

THEY WERE IN THE SAME SCHOOL!

____/1

JOKES TOTAL: ____/4

JESTER 2 CONTINUE TO THE NEXT PAGE →

SiLLY SCENARIOS

(Act it out!)

YOU JUST HAD A LOT OF SUGAR, AND ARE NOW MORE HYPER THAN YOU HAVE EVER BEEN! BOUNCE, ROLL, OR DO ANYTHING ELSE TO GET RID OF ALL THIS ENERGY!

/2

ACT LIKE AN ANGRY GORILLA THAT IS BEATBOXING! TIP: POUND ON YOUR GORILLA CHEST AS PART OF THE BEAT!

/2

SILLY SCENARIOS TOTAL: _____ /4

TIME TO SCORE YOUR POINTS!

 **JESTER 1**

/8

_____

ROUND TOTAL

 **JESTER 2**

/8

_____

ROUND TOTAL

_____

ROUND CHAMPION

ROUND 2

JOKES

HOW DO LIONS START GRACE?

"LET US PREY."

/1

WHY IS ZEUS ALWAYS AT THE CENTER OF ATTENTION?

HE MAKES SURE NO ONE STEALS HIS THUNDER.

/1

WHAT DO KINGS STUDY IN SCHOOL?

THEIR LOYAL SUBJECTS.

/1

WHAT IS A COW'S FAVORITE GAME?

TRUTH OR DAIRY.

/1

JOKES TOTAL: _____ /4

JESTER 1 CONTINUE TO THE NEXT PAGE ➡

SiLLY SCENARiOS

(Act it out!)

HAPPY BiRHTDAY TO YOU! WHiLE TRYiNG TO BLOW OUT THE CANDLES ON YOUR BiRTHDAY CAKE, YOU REALiZE THEY WON'T GO OUT. STAY DETERMiNED AND DO WHATEVER iT TAKES, EVEN iF THAT MEANS BLOWiNG REALLY, REALLY HARD!

/2 _____

YOU REALLY NEED TO CHARGE YOUR PHONE, BUT EVERY TiME YOU TRY TO PLUG iN YOUR CHARGER - YOU GET AN ELECTRiC SHOCK!

/2 _____

SiLLY SCENARIOS TOTAL: _____ /4

NOW, PASS THE BOOK TO JESTER 2!

JOKES

JESTER 2

WHY DO THE KiDS AND THEiR PARENTS ENJOY MARATHONS SO MUCH?

_/1

IT RUNS iN THE FAMiLY!

WHY iS EXERCiSiNG WiTH SOMEONE A GOOD TEST OF YOUR FRiENDSHiP?

_/1

YOU'LL SEE HOW THEY DO THROUGH THiCK AND THiN!

WHY DiD THE TWO CELEBRiTiES BECOME BEST FRiENDS ON THE PLANE?

_/1

THEY GOT ON FAMOUSLY!

HOW DiD EVERYONE KNOW THE TWO STiTCHES WERE FRiENDS?

_/1

THEY WERE SO CLOSELY-KNiT!

JOKES TOTAL: _/4

JESTER 2 CONTiNUE TO THE NEXT PAGE ➜

SiLLY SCENARiOS

(Act it out!)

YOU'VE JUST WON A BATTLE ROYALE! DO THE BEST, MOST POPULAR DANCE LiKE THE ViDEO GAMES!

_____ /2

DiSPLAY FOR EVERYONE YOUR iNCREDiBLE SKiLLS AS THE WORLD'S GREATEST SOCCER PLAYER! HOWEVER, YOUR LEGS DON'T BEND AT THE KNEE. YOUR LEGS MUST BE COMPLETELY STRAiGHT AS YOU SHOW OFF YOUR SOCCER SKiLLS!

_____ /2

SiLLY SCENARiOS TOTAL: _____ /4

TiME TO SCORE YOUR POiNTS!

JESTER 1

/8

ROUND TOTAL

JESTER 2

/8

ROUND TOTAL

ROUND CHAMPION

ROUND 3

JOKES

WHY DiD THE FROG LOSE THE TALENT COMPETITION?

HE TOAD THE WORST JOKES EVER.

/1

WHAT DiD THE ITALIAN CHEF SAY TO THE BOXER?

"HEY! YOU WANT A PIZZA ME?!"

/1

WHAT DiD ONE CAPPUCCINO SAY TO THE OTHER?

"I LiKE YOU A LATTE!"

/1

WHY WERE THE CLOTHES iN THE CLOSET BEST FRIENDS?

THEY LiKED TO "HANG" OUT TOGETHER!

/1

JOKES TOTAL: _____ /4

JESTER 1 CONTINUE TO THE NEXT PAGE ➜

SiLLY SCENARiOS

(Act it out!)

JESTER 1

SOMEONE HAS PRESSED THE "REWiND" BUTTON ON YOUR DAY - GET READY FOR SCHOOL, BUT ALL YOUR ACTiONS AND WORDS ARE iN REVERSE!

_____ /2

YOU'RE A BASEBALL PiTCHER AND YOU WiND UP YOUR ARM TO THROW A PERFECT PiTCH, BUT EVERY TiME YOU'RE ABOUT THROW, YOUR ARM GOES LiMP! KEEP TRYiNG!

_____ /2

SiLLY SCENARiOS TOTAL: _____ /4

 NOW, PASS THE BOOK TO JESTER 2!

25

JOKES

JESTER 2

HOW DOES PETER PAN GET ACROSS WATER?

HE USES A FERRY (FAIRY)!

/1

WHY WAS THE TRUCKER STOPPED WHEN DRIVING THROUGH THE SCHOOL?

HE DIDN'T HAVE A HAUL PASS.

/1

WHAT COMMAND DO YOU GIVE YOUR DOG WHEN IT GETS HURT?

'HEAL.'

/1

WHY DID THE GIRL FLEE THE SNOW GLOBE?

SHE WAS TIRED OF HER WORLD GETTING TURNED UPSIDE DOWN.

/1

JOKES TOTAL: _____ /4

JESTER 2 CONTINUE TO THE NEXT PAGE →

SILLY SCENARIOS

(Act it out!)

YOU ARE A SECRET AGENT AND THE ROOM IS FILLED WITH LASER BEAMS (THAT YOU MUST NOT TOUCH)! STRIKE A POSE AS YOU STEP UNDER AND OVER, MANEUVERING THROUGH EVERY BEAM, LIKE A SECRET SPY!

/2

YOU ARE ENJOYING A PICNIC LUNCH AND CHOWING DOWN ON SOME FOOD WHEN A BUG FLIES RIGHT DOWN YOUR THROAT. PRETEND TO CHOKE AND FLAIL AROUND, UNTIL IT FINALLY SHOOTS OUT AND YOU CAN BREATHE AGAIN!

/2

SILLY SCENARIOS TOTAL: _____ /4

TIME TO SCORE YOUR POINTS! 27

JESTER 1

/8

ROUND TOTAL

JESTER 2

/8

ROUND TOTAL

ROUND
CHAMPION

ROUND
4

JOKES

WHY ARE LUMBERJACKS THE BEST AT ENDING ARGUMENTS?

THEY KNOW WHEN TO BURY THE HATCHET!

/1

WHAT HAS ONE THUMB AND NO WHEELS?

A HITCH-HIKER!

/1

WHY DO PIRATES DROP OUT OF HIGH SCHOOL?

/1

THEY PLAY WAY TOO MUCH HOOK-EY!

WHY WAS THE LION FEELING SO GOOD ABOUT HIMSELF?

HE HAD A LOT OF PRIDE!

/1

JOKES TOTAL: _____ /4

 JESTER 1 CONTINUE TO THE NEXT PAGE ➜

SiLLY SCENARiOS
(Act it out!)

YOU'RE A CLEANiNG ROBOT STUCK iN 'TURBO MODE'. YOU CAN'T STOP SWEEPiNG, DUSTiNG AND VACUUMiNG AT TOP SPEED!

/2

YOU HAVE JUST SCORED THE WiNNiNG TOUCHDOWN FOR YOUR FOOTBALL TEAM! DO YOUR CRAZiEST ViCTORY DANCE... iN REVERSE!

/2

SILLY SCENARIOS TOTAL: _____ /4

 NOW, PASS THE BOOK TO JESTER 2!

JOKES

WHAT DID THE INSPIRATIONAL CLOCK SAY EVERY 60 MINUTES?

"THIS IS HOUR TIME."

_____ /1

WHAT DID THE BROKEN SCALE SAY, WHEN IT WAS EXCITED TO GET FIXED?

"I CAN'T WEIGHT!"

_____ /1

WHY DO SHEEP MAKE FOR TALENTED STORYTELLERS?

THEY'RE GOOD AT SPINNING YARNS.

_____ /1

WHY DID THE TUNA GO ONLINE?

HE WAS FISHING FOR INFORMATION!

_____ /1

JOKES TOTAL: _____ /4

SILLY SCENARIOS

(Act it out!)

YOU ARE A KUNG-FU MASTER THAT LIKES TO DO HIS MORNING WARM-UP WHILE WALKING THE NEIGHBORHOOD. STROLL THROUGH THE STREETS WHILE RANDOMLY HITTING YOUR BEST KUNG-FU MOVES! (TIP: USE SOUND EFFECTS!)

_____ /2

YOU ARE A BULL FACING DOWN A MATADOR. SHE IS WAVING HER RED CAPE, AND YOU ARE READY TO CHARGE!

_____ /2

SILLY SCENARIOS TOTAL: _____ /4

TIME TO SCORE YOUR POINTS! 33

JESTER 1

/8

_____

ROUND TOTAL

JESTER 2

/8

_____

ROUND TOTAL

_____

ROUND
CHAMPION

ROUND 5

JOKES

JESTER 1

HOW DID THEY DESCRIBE THE MAN WHO CLIMBED A MOUNTAIN WITHOUT HIS HANDS?

/1

AN OUTSTANDING FEET.

WHAT COMMAND DO DOGS LOVE DURING EARTHQUAKES?

/1

'SHAKE.'

WHAT DO YOU CALL A HAMSTER THAT TALKS TOO MUCH?

/1

'A VERBAL GERBIL.'

WHY ARE SANDCASTLE BUILDERS SO POPULAR?

/1

THEY HAVE THE BEST PAILS!

JOKES TOTAL: /4

SiLLY SCENARiOS

(Act it out!)

JESTER 1

YOU'VE BEEN INVITED TO AUDITION FOR YOUR FRIEND'S SILENT BAND, SO GIVE THE WORLD'S BEST AIR DRUM SOLO!

_____ /2

YOU'RE WALKING YOUR DOG WHEN IT SUDDENLY STARTS CHASING A SQUIRREL AND PULLING YOU ALL OVER THE PLACE! HOLD ON TIGHT!

_____ /2

SILLY SCENARIOS TOTAL: _____ /4

 NOW, PASS THE BOOK TO JESTER 2!

37

JOKES

HOW COULD YOU TELL THAT THE PEPSI WAS CONFUSED?

IT WAS SODA-LIRIOUS!   /1

WHAT DID THE CHEESE WIN AS A PRIZE?

THE GRATE-EST TROPHY EVER!   /1

WHY WAS THE CAT SUCH A GOOD FRIEND?

IT WAS VERY PURR-SONABLE.   /1

WHAT DOES WILLY WONKA USE TO HELP HIM WALK?

A CANDY CANE.   /1

JOKES TOTAL: /4

JESTER 2 CONTINUE TO THE NEXT PAGE ➔

SILLY SCENARIOS

(Act it out!)

JESTER 2

VERY SLOWLY, BEGIN JUMP ROPING. YOU QUICKLY REALIZE THE ROPE IS GOING OUT OF YOUR CONTROL AND IS SPEEDING UP, FAST! YOU LOOK CONFUSED, WORRIED, AND SCARED AS THE ROPE MAKES YOU JUMP FASTER AND FASTER UNTIL YOU CAN GO NO FASTER! PRETEND TO FALL TO THE GROUND, BREATHING HEAVILY AND EXHAUSTED!

/2

YOU'RE ABOUT TO RUN INTO THE WALL! DO A FOOTBALL SHUFFLE AS YOU TWIRL AND DODGE THE WALL, CHANGING DIRECTION, RUNNING OFF INTO A NEW DIRECTION, AND THEN END WITH A NICE LITTLE VICTORY DANCE!

/2

SILLY SCENARIOS TOTAL: _____ /4

TIME TO SCORE YOUR POINTS!

JESTER 1

/8

ROUND TOTAL

JESTER 2

/8

ROUND TOTAL

ROUND CHAMPION

ROUND
6

JOKES

WHAT IS SANTA'S FAVORITE VEGETABLE?

THE JINGLE BELL PEPPER.

/1

WHAT DO YOU CALL A ROOSTER THAT BOUNCES UP AND DOWN?

'A SPRING CHICKEN.'

/1

HOW DOES 'D' COMMUNICATE WITH 'F'?

THROUGH E-MAIL.

/1

WHY DID THE JUGGLER GET FIRED?

HE DROPPED THE BALL!

/1

JOKES TOTAL: _____ /4

JESTER 1 CONTINUE TO THE NEXT PAGE ➡

SILLY SCENARIOS

(Act it out!)

IMAGINE YOU ARE YOUR FAVORITE SUPERHERO! YOU ARE SURROUNDED BY ENEMIES AND NEED A QUICK GETAWAY. IMITATE THEIR BEST ABILITIES TO GET AWAY - JUMPING, DODGING, ROLLING, ANYTHING THAT CAN GET YOU OUT OF THE CROSSHAIRS!

/2

PRETEND YOU'RE A COWBOY, GALLOPING ALONG ON YOUR HORSE WHEN YOU SUDDENLY SPOT SOME COWS. PULL OUT THAT LASSO AND TRY TO ROPE ONE OF THEM!

/2

SILLY SCENARIOS TOTAL: _____ /4

NOW, PASS THE BOOK TO JESTER 2!

JOKES

WHAT DID THE BREAD SAY WHEN IT GOT TO THE BOTTOM OF THE HILL?

"THAT'S HOW I ROLL!"

/1

WHAT'S THE OPPOSITE OF EASTER?

WESTER.

/1

WHY IS THE SNAIL SO SHY?

HE HASN'T COME OUT OF HIS SHELL!

/1

WHAT'S A BASEBALL PLAYER'S FAVORITE ANIMAL?

A BAT.

/1

JOKES TOTAL: _____ /4

JESTER 2 CONTINUE TO THE NEXT PAGE ➝

SILLY SCENARIOS

(Act it out!)

YOU'RE A SEAL AND YOU KNOW ALL KINDS OF TRICKS, GIVE THE CROWD A SHOW! CLAP YOUR FINS, BALANCE A BALL ON YOUR NOSE, AND MAKE SOME SEAL NOISES!

/2

ACT LIKE A SILLY CRAB BY WALKING SIDEWAYS, THEN HITTING YOUR BEST CRAB KARATE MOVES!

/2

SILLY SCENARIOS TOTAL: _____ /4

TIME TO SCORE YOUR POINTS!

JESTER 1

/8
_____
ROUND TOTAL

JESTER 2

/8
_____
ROUND TOTAL

_____

ROUND
CHAMPION

ROUND

7

JOKES

WHY DO LIBRARIANS NEVER WORRY ABOUT DINNER RESERVATIONS?

THEY ALWAYS BOOK THEM!

/1

HOW WAS THE CHEF TRICKED INTO MAKING AN OMELETTE?

SOMEONE EGGED HIM ON.

/1

WHAT SIZE FRIES DID THE PSYCHIC ORDER?

MEDIUM.

/1

WHY DID THE DOG STOP WORKING?

HE WANTED TO PAWS FOR A BIT.

/1

JOKES TOTAL: _____ /4

JESTER 1 CONTINUE TO THE NEXT PAGE ➡

SiLLY SCENARiOS

(Act it out!)

YOU'RE PLAYiNG GOLF BUT NO MATTER HOW HARD YOU TRY, YOU KEEP MiSSiNG THE GOLF BALL AND HAVE TO START OVER. KEEP TRYiNG UNTiL YOU GIVE UP AND THROW YOUR GOLF CLUB iN THE AiR, DRAMATiCALLY!

_____ /2

ACT LiKE A CHiRPY BiRD PLAYiNG HOPSCOTCH! DO A LiTTLE TAiL WAG ONCE YOU GET TO THE OTHER SiDE!

_____ /2

SiLLY SCENARiOS TOTAL: _____ /4

 NOW, PASS THE BOOK TO JESTER 2!

49

JOKES

WHY iS GLUE SUCH GOOD FRiENDS WiTH PAPER?

THEY ALWAYS STiCK TOGETHER!

_____ /1

WHAT iS A PARK RANGER'S FAVORiTE DESSERT?

CHOCOLATE MOUSSE.

_____ /1

WHAT DO YOU CALL A SEE-SAW WiTH ONE SiDE?

BROKEN.

_____ /1

WHAT DO BABiES RiDE TO GET RiD OF THEiR DiAPERS?

THE POTTY TRAiN.

_____ /1

JOKES TOTAL: _____ /4

SILLY SCENARIOS

(Act it out!)

LAY DOWN ON YOUR BACK AND DO THE 'YMCA' WITH ONLY YOUR LEGS!

/2

YOU ARE THE KING OF THE JUNGLE! KEEPING YOUR FEET ON THE FLOOR, BEND AT THE WAIST UNTIL YOUR HANDS TOUCH THE GROUND. NOW WALK ON ALL FOURS LIKE THE LION YOU ARE AND END WITH A GIANT ROAR!

/2

SILLY SCENARIOS TOTAL: _____ /4

TIME TO SCORE YOUR POINTS!

JESTER 1

/8

ROUND TOTAL

JESTER 2

/8

ROUND TOTAL

ROUND
CHAMPION

ROUND

8

JOKES

WHAT MAKES PEOPLE OF THE SAME HEIGHT BECOME FRIENDS?

THEY CAN SEE EYE TO EYE!

/1

WHAT DID THE CANDLE SAY TO THE FIRE?

"YOU'VE MET YOUR MATCH!"

/1

WHY DO BASEBALL PLAYERS MAKE GOOD MUSIC?

BECAUSE THEY'RE ALWAYS CRANKING OUT THE HITS.

/1

WHY WAS THE COMPUTER A BAD DRIVER?

IT WAS ALWAYS CRASHING!

/1

JOKES TOTAL: _____ /4

 JESTER 1 CONTINUE TO THE NEXT PAGE ➡

SiLLY SCENARiOS

(Act it out!)

JESTER 1

YOUR RiGHT HAND SUDDENLY HAS A MiND OF iTS OWN AND WANTS TO TiCKLE YOU, POKE YOU AND PiCK YOUR NOSE! USE ALL YOUR STRENGTH TO TRY AND FiGHT BACK.

/2

BECOME AN OPERA-SiNGiNG YODELER. BELT OUT THOSE YODELS WHiLE MAKiNG GRAND HAND GESTURES.

/2

SiLLY SCENARiOS TOTAL: _____ /4

NOW, PASS THE BOOK TO JESTER 2!

JOKES

I TRIED TO ADD COLOR TO A BALLOON WITH A COLORED PENCIL. IT REALLY MADE IT POP!   /1

WHAT DO YOU CALL A SNEAKY MOUNTAIN?

'A PEAK.'   /1

WHAT LIES BUT ALSO TELLS THE TRUTH?

THE LIE-BRARY!   /1

WHY AREN'T CARNIVALS TAKEN SERIOUSLY?

THEY'RE ALWAYS CLOWNING AROUND!   /1

JOKES TOTAL: /4

JESTER 2 CONTINUE TO THE NEXT PAGE ➜

SILLY SCENARIOS

(Act it out!)

ACT LIKE AN OLD TURKEY WALKING WITH A CANE. DON'T FORGET TO GOBBLE, GOBBLE!

/2

YOU ARE THE NEWEST ROBOT DOG ON THE MARKET, AND YOU HAVE BEEN PROGRAMMED WITH THE MOST AMAZING TRICKS! YOU JUST MET YOUR NEW OWNER, SO IMPRESS THEM WITH ALL THE COOL ROBOT DOG TRICKS!

/2

SILLY SCENARIOS TOTAL: _____ /4

TIME TO SCORE YOUR POINTS!

JESTER 1

/8

ROUND TOTAL

JESTER 2

/8

ROUND TOTAL

ROUND
CHAMPION

ROUND

9

JOKES

WHY DiD NOBODY LiKE THE REFEREE?

HE SMELLED FOUL.

/1

WHAT DiD THE BLANKET SAY WHEN THE BED ASKED FOR HELP?

"I GOT iT COVERED."

/1

WHAT DO YOU CALL iT WHEN YOU PUT TWO FiNGERS ON A TABLE?

A HANDSTAND.

/1

WHAT DO YOU CALL A TRAiN THAT iS ALWAYS SNEEZiNG?

/1

'A-CHOO-CHOO!'

JOKES TOTAL: _____ /4

JESTER 1 CONTINUE TO THE NEXT PAGE ➜

SiLLY SCENARiOS

(Act it out!)

MAKE A SiLLY OR CRAZY FACE, BALANCE ON ONE LEG, AND STAY FROZEN LiKE THAT. EVERY TiME YOU BLiNK YOU HAVE TO CHANGE YOUR SiLLY FACE TO A DiFFERENT SiLLY FACE, SWiTCH FEET, AND MAKE A LOUD NON-SENSiCAL SOUND. BLiNK AS FEW TiMES AS POSSiBLE!

_____ /2

YOU'RE A BiG BEAR AND YOUR BACK iS SO iTCHY, BUT YOU CAN'T REACH iT. FiND A GOOD, TALL TREE TO SCRATCH YOUR BACK AGAiNST AND GO TO TOWN!

_____ /2

SILLY SCENARIOS TOTAL: _____ /4

 NOW, PASS THE BOOK TO JESTER 2!

61

JOKES

WHAT IS SPONGEBOB'S FAVORITE WORD?

"SQUID-WORD!"

_____ /1

HOW DO YOU KNOW THAT THE OCEAN IS FRIENDLY?

IT ALWAYS WAVES!

_____ /1

HOW DOES AN ANGRY TEA KETTLE CALM DOWN?

IT JUST LETS OFF A LITTLE STEAM.

_____ /1

WHAT'S THE FASTEST WAY TO SEE YOUR GRANDMA?

JUST USE INSTA-GRAM!

_____ /1

JOKES TOTAL: _____ /4

JESTER 2 CONTINUE TO THE NEXT PAGE ➤

SILLY SCENARIOS

(Act it out!)

YOU'RE A HAPPY CLOWN PERFORMING TRICKS AT A PARTY, BUT YOU TRIP AND HIT YOUR HEAD. WHEN YOU WAKE UP, YOU'VE CHANGED INTO A CRAZY CLOWN CHASING EVERYONE!

/2

SHOW HOW A KANGAROO WOULD PLAY BASKETBALL!

/2

SILLY SCENARIOS TOTAL: _____ /4

TIME TO SCORE YOUR POINTS!

JESTER 1

/8
_____
ROUND TOTAL

JESTER 2

/8
_____
ROUND TOTAL

_____

ROUND CHAMPION

ROUND

10

JOKES

WHY DID THE CHEESE GET AN AWARD?

IT DID A GOUDA JOB!

/1

WHAT DO SMARTPHONES DOWNLOAD WHEN THEY ARE HUNGRY?

APP-ETIZERS.

/1

WHY IS HUMPTY DUMPTY HAPPY THAT SUMMER IS OVER?

SO HE CAN HAVE A GREAT FALL!

/1

WHAT FLOWER NEVER TELLS THE TRUTH?

A LIE-LAC.

/1

JOKES TOTAL: _____ /4

SILLY SCENARIOS

(Act it out!)

YOU HAVE PHONOPHOBIA (FEAR OF LOUD NOISES), BUT YOU ALSO LOVE TO CLAP!

/2

YOU FIND YOURSELF IN EGYPT AMONG THE PYRAMIDS. TRY AND FIT IN BY DOING YOUR BEST 'WALK LIKE AN EGYPTIAN' DANCE IMPRESSION!

/2

SILLY SCENARIOS TOTAL: _____ /4

NOW, PASS THE BOOK TO JESTER 2!

JOKES

WHY COULDN'T THE BOOK STAND UP FOR ITSELF?

IT HAD NO SPINE!

/1

WHAT KIND OF CELEBRATION IS HELD IN THE BATHROOM?

A BIRTHDAY POTTY!

/1

WHAT FLOWER LIKES TO TELL JOKES?

A SILLY LILY.

/1

WHAT DO YOU CALL A STINKY COMPUTER?

A COM-PEE-YU-TER.

/1

JOKES TOTAL: /4

JESTER 2 CONTINUE TO THE NEXT PAGE ➜

SILLY SCENARIOS

(Act it out!)

JESTER 2

YOU'RE A DOG WHO CAN'T FIND HIS BONE.
KEEP DIGGING HOLES UNTIL YOU FIND IT!

_____ /2

IT IS A DANCE PARTY AND YOUR TURN TO LET
EVERYONE SEE YOUR DANCE SKILLS. SADLY, YOU ARE
STUCK IN SUPER SLOW MOTION! MAKE SURE TO
INCLUDE MANY POPULAR DANCE MOVES (FLOSSING,
DISCO, AND MORE), BUT KEEP IT SLOW!

_____ /2

SILLY SCENARIOS TOTAL: _____ /4

TIME TO SCORE YOUR POINTS!

JESTER 1

/8
_____
ROUND TOTAL

JESTER 2

/8
_____
ROUND TOTAL

_____

ROUND
CHAMPION

ADD UP ALL YOUR POINTS FROM EACH ROUND.
THE PLAYER WITH THE MOST POINTS IS CROWNED
THE ULTIMATE LAUGH MASTER!

IN THE EVENT OF A TIE, CONTINUE TO THE ROUND
11 FOR THE TIE-BREAKER ROUND!

 JESTER 1 _____
GRAND TOTAL

 JESTER 2 _____
GRAND TOTAL

_____
THE ULTIMATE
DON'T LAUGH CHALLENGE MASTER

ROUND

11

TIE-BREAKER
(WINNER TAKES ALL!)

JOKES

WHAT MADE THE TWO CHARACTERS THINK THEY WERE GOING TO BE BEST FRIENDS?

THEY WERE ALWAYS ON THE SAME PAGES!

/1

WHY DO BEANS AND CORN NEVER FEEL SAFE?

THEY'RE ALWAYS BEING STALKED!

/1

HOW DO YOU KNOW THAT TRIANGLES ARE SMART?

WELL, THEY DO HAVE 180 DEGREES!

/1

WHAT DO TREES DO FOR GOOD LUCK?

KNOCK ON WOOD.

/1

JOKES TOTAL: _____ /4

 JESTER 1 CONTINUE TO THE NEXT PAGE ➡

SiLLY SCENARIOS

(Act it out!)

DO YOUR BEST iMPRESSION OF YOURSELF SiNGiNG iN THE SHOWER WHiLE WASHiNG YOUR HAiR, BUT WiTHOUT SOUND! AND DON'T FORGET TO DANCE LiKE NO ONE iS WATCHiNG!

/2

SLOTHS ALWAYS MOVE SO SLOW, BUT LOOK SO HAPPY! ACT LiKE A LAZY SLOTH DOiNG THE LiMBO! HOW LOW CAN YOU GO?

/2

SILLY SCENARIOS TOTAL: _____ /4

NOW, PASS THE BOOK TO JESTER 2!

JOKES

WHY DID THE DOLPHINS BECOME BEST FRIENDS?

THEY GOT ON SWIMMINGLY!

/1

WHY SHOULD BEST FRIENDS WEAR SHIRTS MADE OF TISSUES?

SO THEY CAN BE A SHOULDER TO CRY ON!

/1

WHY IS FOOD YOUR BEST FRIEND?

IT KNOWS YOU INSIDE AND OUT!

/1

WHY ARE ALL CAROUSEL ANIMALS FRIENDS?

THEY TRAVEL IN THE SAME CIRCLES!

/1

JOKES TOTAL: _____ /4

JESTER 2 CONTINUE TO THE NEXT PAGE ➜

SILLY SCENARIOS

(Act it out!)

YOU ARE TAKING A STROLL IN THE PARK WHEN YOU DECIDE TO SIT DOWN. PLOP, DOWN YOU SIT, WHEN YOU REALIZE YOU HAVE SAT IN SOMETHING NASTY AND IT IS ALL OVER YOU NOW! FRANTICALLY, YOU TRY TO GET THE GOOP OFF OF YOURSELF, YOUR CLOTHES, AND YOUR SHOES. EW, IT'S EVEN IN YOUR HAIR!

_____ /2

YOU ARE TRAPPED IN A BOX THAT KEEPS SHRINKING AND SHRINKING. STRIKE A STURDY POSE TO KEEP THE WALLS FROM CAVING IN AND CRUSHING YOU TO THE FLOOR!

_____ /2

SILLY SCENARIOS TOTAL: _____ /4

TIME TO SCORE YOUR POINTS!

ADD UP ALL YOUR POINTS FROM THE PREVIOUS ROUND. THE JESTER WITH THE MOST POINTS IS CROWNED THE ULTIMATE DON'T LAUGH CHALLENGE MASTER!

JESTER 1

/8

GRAND TOTAL

JESTER 2

/8

GRAND TOTAL

THE ULTIMATE
DON'T LAUGH CHALLENGE MASTER

Check out our

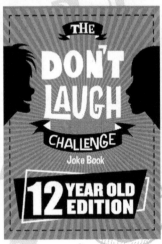

Visit us at
www.DontLaughChallenge.com
to check out our newest books!

other joke books!

If you have enjoyed our book, we would love for you to review us on Amazon!

Made in the USA
Middletown, DE
20 December 2019

81505426R00046